IT'S TIME TO EAT DATES

It's Time to Eat DATES

Walter the Educator

Silent King Books
A WhichHead Entertainment Imprint

Copyright © 2024 by Walter the Educator

All rights reserved. No part of this book may be reproduced in any manner whatsoever without written per- mission except in the case of brief quotations embodied in critical articles and reviews.

First Printing, 2024

Disclaimer

This book is a literary work; the story is not about specific persons, locations, situations, and/or circumstances unless mentioned in a historical context. Any resemblance to real persons, locations, situations, and/or circumstances is coincidental. This book is for entertainment and informational purposes only. The author and publisher offer this information without warranties expressed or implied. No matter the grounds, neither the author nor the publisher will be accountable for any losses, injuries, or other damages caused by the reader's use of this book. The use of this book acknowledges an understanding and acceptance of this disclaimer.

It's Time to Eat DATES is a collectible early learning book by Walter the Educator suitable for all ages belonging to Walter the Educator's Time to Eat Book Series. Collect more books at WaltertheEducator.com

USE THE EXTRA SPACE TO TAKE NOTES AND DOCUMENT YOUR MEMORIES

DATES

It's time to eat a tasty treat,

It's Time to Eat

Dates

A little snack that's oh so sweet!

Brown and shiny, smooth and small,

Dates are here to please us all.

They grow on trees, so very tall,

In sunny places, that's their call.

Picked with care by gentle hands,

They come to us from desert lands.

Soft and chewy, what a delight,

A snack to share, day or night.

Full of goodness, so they say,

They give us energy to play.

Pop one in and take a bite,

The flavor's rich, it feels just right!

Sticky fingers, oh, what fun,

You'll want another when you're done.

It's Time to Eat

Dates

They're good alone or in a dish,

In cookies, pies, or as you wish.

Chop them up or eat them whole,

Dates are food that warm the soul.

For lunch, for snacks, or breakfast too,

There's so much that dates can do.

They're nature's candy, don't you see?

A yummy gift for you and me!

If you feel a little slow,

Eat some dates, and off you'll go!

With every bite, you'll start to see,

How dates can fill you with energy.

So thank the trees, and thank the sun,

For making dates for everyone.

A little fruit that's big with cheer,

It's Time to Eat
Dates

Let's all enjoy them far and near!

Packed with love and vitamins too,

Dates are a gift that's just for you.

So when you're hungry, grab a few,

They're healthy, tasty, and good as new!

It's time to eat a tasty treat,

A little snack that's oh so sweet!

Brown and shiny, smooth and small,

It's Time to Eat
Dates

Dates are here to please us all.

ABOUT THE CREATOR

Walter the Educator is one of the pseudonyms for Walter Anderson. Formally educated in Chemistry, Business, and Education, he is an educator, an author, a diverse entrepreneur, and he is the son of a disabled war veteran. "Walter the Educator" shares his time between educating and creating. He holds interests and owns several creative projects that entertain, enlighten, enhance, and educate, hoping to inspire and motivate you. Follow, find new works, and stay up to date with Walter the Educator™

at WaltertheEducator.com

www.ingramcontent.com/pod-product-compliance
Lightning Source LLC
LaVergne TN
LVHW052011060526
838201LV00059B/3980